TRAUMATIC BLESSINGS

ROLAND M. TENNYSON

TRAUMATIC BLESSINGS

Roland M. Tennyson

Kravitz & Sons

INNOVATORS IN PUBLISHING, MARKETING AND ADVERTISING

Kravitz and Sons LLC
204 E Arlington Blvd. Suite B
Greenville, NC 27858

Published by Kravitz and Sons LLC.

ISBN: 979-8-89639-739-7 (sc)
ISBN: 979-8-89639-738-0 (e)

Library of Congress Control Number: 2026908405

Table Of Contents

CHAPTER 1

"THE COMA"

This experience was truly a blessing, in the coma there was a voice that spoke to me, the voice was deep and soothing, very comforting. I didn't know what was going on. The first thing this voice said was "Jazail", this voice called me Jazail. The next thing that happened kind of startled me, the voice said look and as I raised my head, I saw a car on the road, it was the car that my family traveled in on our way home from out of town.

I saw everybody in the car, including myself (that was scary). So, I asked," What is this"? The voice said, "This is a blessing". It was kind of strange cause I had no idea what he was talking about. As I watched, I saw my dad; he didn't look too well, he was sweating, and he started to blink his eyes a lot. My mom was sleeping in the front seat.

His head fell onto the steering wheel, and the car swerved and hit the concrete divider on the highway. My dad was out of cold, and his body was lifeless. His arms turned the wheel when his body shifted when the side of the car hit the concrete divider, and right then, we hit the back of a tractor-trailer. My mom, who was in the front seat, hit the windshield and then hit the dashboard. My nephew Terry went forward and hit the stereo, and all that part of the front compartment (Terry was sitting in the middle on the back seat), which caused extensive bone trauma to his face, and his leg got crushed when he went forward, causing his leg to be broken in three places.

My brother looked in disbelief as he saw our mother hurt and unresponsive, and me hurt and unresponsive. Didn't know whether we were dead or alive? My brother looked at Terry, who was very hysterical, and noticed that Terry had a huge hole right below the bridge of his nose. It was nasty, every time Terry would scream bloody snot and mucous would blow out of this hole in his nose. Malcolm was still in shock.

My brother then stood up cause the roof of the car was gone, ripped off when we hit the truck. My brother then looked down at our father and saw that the top of his head was gone, the hood of the car came back through the windshield and took the top of our father's head off, he died instantly.

Now my brother, still unbelieved, never once checked to make sure he himself was all right. After seeing all this, my brother sat down and started to cry, and at the same time was trying to calm Terry down. I don't know what time of day it was, but it was dark. Soon after, two vehicles stopped to get us some help and they called for help. I'm watching this from above as if I was watching from the sky. I saw a lot of lights and a helicopter landing near the accident.

Then I was in the dark, looking at a bright figure but I couldn't see who it was because the figure I saw was so bright. The voice then said, "Now you know", and I said, "know what, am I dead?" He said, "no, you have seen what has happened, you and your family did not make it back home safely and your father is no longer of this world." I responded and said, "who are you?" "Where am I?" He said, "I am who I am, your strength now and always and whenever you feel alone and scared or maybe confused just tell Me what's on your heart and I will comfort you."

"Your choice is simple, awake and live for the purpose of serving or sleeping and be patient for judgment will come." "Sleep and that is it, your chance for experience will be gone, but awake and live and I will give you experiences unlike any other, for this experience alone is remarkable."

"Your life will be great, your road will be rough, but I will not allow more than you can bear, also when you speak of your life, many will not believe your experience with me." I responded and asked, "what then can I do?"

"What can I say to make them believe?" You said, "tell them to look at you, you are one of my many blessings to this earth." "Your world is not this earth, this earth is a part of your world, it is as real as I am." "It's not for those who will hear but for those who will listen."

Chapter 2

"Awakening"

I slowly opened my eyes. Memories of things before that moment were gone, erased, and I didn't like where I was, so I started to scream, but nothing came out, no sound at all. I had tubes in my nose, Iv's in my hands, stickers on my chest, and who are all these people surrounding me, and happy to see me awake. I didn't know where I was, and really, I didn't know anything except the vision. Next, I remember getting very combative, my iv's, I ripped out of my hands, and the tubes in my nose, I pulled those out, and the stickers, well those were pulled off too. Eventually, the nurses and doctors came in and first tried to calm me down, but later I remember being held down and then tied to bed with restraints, they tied me down I think to keep me from hurting myself.

I think I went back to sleep after that. When I woke up, my brother was there. I think he had other people with him, but I'm not sure. I really don't remember what we did, but I do remember him untying me, and when he did, I pulled those tubes out of my nose again and again, and I was tied down to the bed. My brother talked to me, asking me if I remembered anything and I don't know why but I repeated those exact words back to him, every time My brother would say something to me I would say those exact words back to him, for example: he would say, "Roland, how are you doing?" And I would say, "Roland, how are you doing?" I almost felt brand new, like I had to start life all over again. My brother came around a lot in the beginning, but every time I saw him, he would ask me the same questions, wanting to know if I remembered anything and if I knew where I was and why I was there.

I remember Sharmane coming to see me when I was in the intensive care unit where I woke up. Sharmane was my sister Ruthie's best friend at the time, and for some reason I remember Sharmane coming to see me in the hospital, but I don't remember my sister Ruthie coming to see me, but anyway I remember Sharmane giving me a hug and saying," how are you feeling today, Roland?" And I said the exact words back to her, "how are you feeling today, Roland?" And she looked at my brother and said, "Why did he say the same thing back to me, should I be talking to him right now?" My brother said, "He's just Waking up and the doctors said he may never be the same again, but that it was too early to tell but that Roland would be taken to Holmes hospital for rehabilitation, and there they would be able to perform more tests, but the doctor also said that they should prepare for the worst because the test that were already performed didn't look too good and that it looks like Roland has brain damage."

Chapter 3

"Rehabilitation"

Time went on and I was taken to Holmes hospital for rehab; there I went into my bedroom and for some reason my nurse looked a lot like my Grandmother (my dad's mother). After I settled in, I remember being very quiet and even though people would come into my room and try to talk to me I would remain quiet. I do remember talking to my nurse who looked just like my Grandmother. She took me for walks sometimes to get out of the hospital; we would go to McDonald's sometimes and sometimes we would just go to the park.

My nurse told me one day that she didn't like the way I was breathing and that it seemed to get worse the more I walked. My nurse eventually contacted the Ear, Nose, and Throat (E.N.T) doctors at Cincinnati Children's Hospital where they took me after evaluating me at Holmes Hospital. Soon after that, I met Dr. Robin Cotton who had an English accent and wasn't much taller than me at that time. Dr. Cotton is the doctor in charge; he did all my throat and airway operations. I remember my first operation; it was called an endoscope. This procedure would allow Dr. Cotton to see my airway to figure out why I was having trouble breathing. After the operation, Dr. Cotton informed my family that my airway was narrow and that it was kind of complicated because both my upper and lower airways were narrow, about the size of an infant's airway.

Chapter 4

LIFE WITH THE T-TUBE

Dr. Cotton informed them that he would need to operate and place a tracheostomy tube in my throat, he would later explain that the tracheotomy he would need to place in my airway was unlike normal tracheostomies, because both my upper and lower airways were narrow, so the tube he said he would need to place is called a T-tube because it is shaped like a -T- to open both my upper and lower airways.

I also had to go back to Holmes Hospital for rehab because doctors there seemed to believe that I had an organic mental disorder, they said I was mentally retarded and that I had brain damage, and also that I would never read past a third-grade level, so in the midst of all this, I did the only thing I knew to do and that was pray. My Mom was hospitalized, and my dad was killed, something I knew that my family had no idea I knew. They all came to my room at Holmes Hospital, my aunts and uncles, brothers and sisters and they told me that my Dad had died in a car accident. They told me my Dad didn't make it, something I already knew. I looked at them without saying a word, without facial expression, because I already knew. My aunt came to hug me, she said, "Roland, it's o.k. to cry," and still I said nothing. My reaction was blank; I just knew not to say a word.

Soon after they left, I called for my nurse, Grandma, because she looked so much like my Grandmother. Eventually, the doctors in rehab didn't give me much of a chance of improving mentally, so they sent me back to the Children's

Hospital so that there would be no interruptions in my physical treatment.

When I got back to the Children's Hospital, I spent the next ten months or more there, in and out of surgery before I was allowed to go home for the first time, but that didn't last long because soon after I got home my health started to get worse so I was readmitted to Children's Hospital, and this time in the hospital, I was taken to surgery so much that I started to feel like a science project. I started to pray more and more every day.

Now that the T-tube was on. I had to take classes just to learn how to take care of it. This T-tube made life for me very difficult, because everywhere I went I had to take a suction machine with me, and right out in public I had to use this loud suction machine to suction my T-tube out. The nurses there were very informative, they explained a lot, but I was still young, about 12 or 13 y.o, and if doctors at Holmes Hospital gave me such a bad mental diagnosis why they thought that I would be able to take care of such a complicated thing, and Even though my sister Marsha learned to care for my T-tube every time I needed to be suctioned, she would make me do it.

I was in the hospital quite a bit at this time in my life. I was in the hospital so much that it practically became my home. The nurses took care of me so well in the hospital; I was treated better in the hospital than I was at home.

It was almost a way of life, me in the hospital. As a matter of fact, that was my life. Surgery after surgery, procedure after procedure, this is all I knew, or my first experiences after I woke up from the coma.

When I got out of the hospital, I would go home for a while but then for some reason or another I would have to go back to the hospital for more surgery, I mean that happened so much that heard that most of my family, if not all of them, felt that I was faking everything. I don't know how someone who spent ten weeks in a coma and was diagnosed with mental disorders at the age I was could fake such a thing but that's what I found out my family was telling everyone; we'll be all my family except my Mom and my two brothers Donald and Riley who were away in the military. I guess that's why I got very little support from them (aunts and uncles, brothers and sisters) and I tell you that shows what my family thought of me.

There were times when I would complain of pain or shortness of breath and my sisters would go shopping or something else to blow me off, but she did take me to the hospital when she got back home (Boy was she concerned).

Now that I was back in the hospital, with more surgeries, more procedures, and some results, my airways were narrowing again. There must be something else that can be done.

This airway problem went on for years and every time Dr. Cotton removed the T-tube my airway would collapse, so Dr. Cotton gave my sister Marsha some options for my treatment. All decisions about my treatment were made by my sister Marsha because she became my legal guardian while our mother was sick.

Dr. Cotton gave Marsha two options for my treatment. One, he could place the T-tube and leave it in permanently, or Two, he could perform a procedure called a tracheal resection, where he would have to crack my chest open to gain access to my airway so that he could cut or resect the narrow parts of my airway, and because the airway stretches, he would be able to Sew or mend the other two open areas in my airway back together so that I would not have to live with the T-tube for the rest of my life.

Let me give you a little history on the T-tube to let you know why it was important to not have to live with it all my life. The T-tube is designed for the sole purpose of opening both upper and lower airways. T-tubes were very rarely used because it is a very rare circumstance where both upper and lower airways narrow at the same time. Most tracheostomies are designed to open either the upper or lower airway requiring these types to have trachea ties to hold it in place in the airway. The T-tube did not require trachea ties because in surgery and the way it is designed is that once the T-tube is placed in the airway the tube is inflated keeping it in place. With the other tracheostomies you suction either up or down, but with the T-tube you had to suction both up and down.

To suction up you had to press down on the tube, the part that was sticking out of the front of the neck and to suction down you had to lift on the T-tube. In most cases, you cannot speak when you have a tracheostomy tube in your throat because you have an opening in your throat, but with the T-tube I was able to speak because I had a plug that fit right at the end of my T-tube which plugged the opening in my airway and I could easily remove the plug to suction the T-tube out to clean it.

So now you see why it was such an important thing for me not to have to live with this for the rest of my life, I mean this was a lot of responsibility for someone so young. So after Dr. Cotton explained to Marsha how risky this operation was she came to me to talk to me about how I felt about it and for the most part I was just happy that there was a way for me not to have to live with this T-tube for the rest of my life, but I was scared about getting my chest cut open so I prayed about it and God gave me comfort. I think Marsha saw the responsibility and how much she would have to do if I did have to have the T-Tube long-term, but I am so blessed to have had Marsha there to do what she did for me. Dr. Cotton told Marsha that this type of operation was rare and very rarely done, he also explained to Marsha that the risk for serious infection and complications was very high which could lead to death, but the decision was made to go ahead with the operation.

CHAPTER 5

"THE PREPARATION"

Now that the decision was made as to what type of treatment I would have, a lot of preparation followed. At least two to three months of preparation. They had to take pictures of this part of my chest and that part of my chest, and a lot of blood tests, it was a very intense time. Then Dr. Cotton had to decide which cardiothoracic surgeon he would hire to open my chest so that he could operate.

As time went on, I began to become more and more nervous, I knew what was going to happen and it was no longer just another operation, they were going to cut my chest open. A scary thought, yes, but I knew that GOD was in control and that my life was in God's hands and that the doctors, though very skilled in their craft, were being used on my behalf.

So as the day drew closer and closer I found myself praying a lot just telling God how I felt and what I didn't feel. I knew that this was just the beginning of a long road to recovery and though I had no idea of the specifics of my journey I did know that my Heavenly Father would be there to protect me every step of the way.

CHAPTER 6

"The Night Before"

24 hours, yes one day away from major surgery. Me and my nephew Terry talked a lot. He was my best friend. We were raised together. Terry told me how when we were in the hospital and I was in the coma he would ask his nurse to take him to where I was in the hospital so that he could read to me while I was sleeping, he told me about flying in the helicopter when we were taken to the hospital after the accident he said that they put us in the helicopter to get us to the hospital faster and I told him that I don't remember that and he said that's because I was sleep. I prayed for peace, and calm nerves because I was very nervous.

I had to wake up at 4:00 in the morning because I had to be at the hospital by 5 am to get prepared for surgery that was scheduled for 6 or 6:15 am.

I was extremely hungry because the night before surgery I was not allowed to eat anything.

CHAPTER 7

"The Day of Surgery"

So, the day is finally here and so far, I'm pretty secure in knowing that God is in control and that I will be just fine. It is now six o'clock in the morning and the nurse is preparing to give me an IV and at this point needles aren't that big a deal to me right now because I've been stuck so many times with needles up to this point that I almost I guess have become immune to the pain not to mention everything else that was on my mind at the time.

The surgery time was rescheduled for seven fifteen so now I have to wait even longer to eat. I am now all ready to go under the knife for my first major operation and I am getting very nervous, so I started to pray. I know that after the nurse started my IV, I was told that it would be about an hour before I went into surgery.

Some doctors came in to see me before I went into the operating room, they said that they were Dr. Cotton's fellows which I would learn later on that they were a part of Dr. Cotton's medical team, they just came in and introduced themselves and explained to me a little about the operation and who they were, the anesthesiologist said that he was in charge of putting me to sleep and keeping me asleep while the doctors do the operation and also told me and my family what we should expect after I wake up.

It is now seven o'clock and they are ready for me in the operating room, so we had a word of prayer, and I was taken to the operating room. Once I was in the operating room Dr. Cotton came to me and said that everything would be just fine and that I was in good hands (I guess he must have known about my prayer).

CHAPTER 8

"AFTER THE OPERATION"

Once I was on the operating table I was hooked on to a lot of machines. They put stickers on my chest, and they hooked my IV up to something and I heard a lot of beeping. They put an oxygen mask over my face that smelled like bubblegum and they told me to tell them my favorite food, and I started to get very light-headed and the room started spinning and all those beeps I heard before got very loud and before I knew it I was asleep.

I woke up in the p.a.c.u or the recovery room after surgery, my nurse told me that the surgery went well from what she heard and that I would be spending the night recovering and then I would be taken to the intensive care unit where I would spend at least a week.

I remember it being dark when I came into the hospital because it was so early in the morning and now that I was out of surgery it was still dark so I figured that the surgery must not have taken too long so I asked the nurse, "how long did the operation take? It was still dark outside?" And that's when she said that when I came in for surgery it was morning time but now it was nighttime, so I guess the operation was kind of lengthy.

I had a tube in my nose for feeding and a tube in my chest to drain fluid or blood and I had three Iv's, one in both hands and one in my foot. When the IV was taken out of my foot it hurt so bad I couldn't walk for a week. Having an IV on your foot is very painful. I did spend a week in intensive care before they sent me to a regular floor.

About two or three days after the surgery a doctor came into the room and said that he was there to remove my chest tube, so I asked him, "aren't you going to put me to sleep first?" He said, "no, it shouldn't hurt." He just told me to take a deep breath in, and it would be over before I knew it and he was right. The doctor then said that he had to remove the staples from my chest, which was a surprise because I had no idea I had staples in my chest, so I told him, "I know you're going to put me to sleep for this." The doctor said, "no it shouldn't hurt at all." I said, "o.k. how are you going to do this?" He said, "if your nervous, close your eyes and let me take out one staple and if it does not hurt that I would let him remove the rest of the staples."

So, I said, "Deal" and closed my eyes. About fifteen seconds later the doctor said, "o.k. you can open your eyes." I said, "wow, I didn't feel that at all, alright you can take the rest of the staples out." The doctor said, "Too late, they're already gone." He tricked me, he took all of them out while my eyes were closed, he was good.

CHAPTER 9

"HOME, BUT NOT HEALED"

Now when I went to the floor I was expecting some of my family to be there, but no one was there and I cried because I didn't think they loved me. They came when it was time for me to go home.

I was happy to go home because my nephew Terry was there, me and my nephew were best friends and when I went home, I had someone to play with, my sister Ruthie and my brother Malcolm weren't very sociable with me at this time.

Terry and I were close mainly because we were raised together. Terry is my nephew, but we are the same age, I am just eleven days older than he is. Since my sister was young when Terry was born, Terry came to live with my family since my parents are his grandparents.

I always thought Terry was my brother, it wasn't until we were older that I found out that I was actually his uncle, but he never called me uncle, but I didn't care because we were best friends. Terry and I liked to sing. We would sing together and we even had some friends from the neighborhood sing with us sometimes we had a singing group kinda like Boyz II Men. Boyz ii Men was my favorite singing group I Loved the way they sing and harmonize I never heard anything like it before but Terry's favorite group was Envogue, he was in love with that group but anyway me and Terry and our friends loved to go to a place called Americana an amusement park in Ohio we would stand at the gate when people were coming in and sing Boyz ii Men songs and Shai songs and Silk songs just music we liked to listen to at home people would complement our singing and throw us money mostly change though like quarters and dimes we had fun.

We also loved to play video games on our Nintendo our favorites were mario brother and zelda. We would have tournaments in Mario kart that were fun and also mortal combat, but I didn't like mortal combat because Terry was the best and I would always lose. We were young and I remember one day me and Terry were out with Preston and William, two friends that we sang and played with. We came across this store that bought old CDs and video games. Me and Terry later that day went to a grocery store called Biggs at forest fair mall with my sister Marsha and saw that Biggs had a big box of old cd's and video games right in the middle of the store for sale so he suggested we take some and sell them at the buyback store so we agreed Me, Terry and William one of our singing partners and we were good at it until we got caught about a month later we had to see a judge and everything we had community service and probation that was the dumbest thing I ever did. Me and Terry had a lot of fun together though riding our bikes and fishing and walking everywhere we were best friends.

CHAPTER 10

"BACK TO THE HOSPITAL"

About three months after I came home this time from the hospital, once again my airway collapsed again and again I was admitted into children's hospital where I was seen by Dr. Cotton again, this time when he took me to surgery I woke up in intensive care, but this time I had a large light blue tube in my nose, they said that it was placed through my vocal cords so I couldn't even talk. I was told that my airway had collapsed so the doctors would have to operate again and that the tube in my nose was there to keep my airway open until Dr. Cotton decided what he was going to do. I started praying, talking to my heavenly father was my way of finding peace in the middle of this storm. After I prayed, I just knew that I would be just fine.

Dr. Cotton met with my sister Marsha again and said that there were two options, he could place the T-tube back in my airway and leave it there permanently or he could open my chest again and try to remove the narrow area of my airway again as he did the first time.

My sister told me what the options were and that she felt that she would rather go with the open chest operation again because she didn't feel like being responsible for my T-tube again if she didn't have to. So once again I was scheduled for another open chest operation. I had to spend about two weeks in intensive care while the doctors prepared for the operation.

Finally, they decided exactly when to do the operation again. I went back to surgery again and this operation took about ten to twelve hours and again my chest was cut open and again my chest was stapled closed, once again I had a tube in my chest and again I had a feeding tube in my nose and two IV's. I spent about a week and a half in intensive care this time and I began to think about how tired I was of constantly going to surgery. I started praying and just asking God how much more, when would all this pain end.

CHAPTER 11

"FEELING ALONE"

So, after spending my time in intensive care I went back to the floor where I had to spend another week before I could go home. I started to feel so alone. My Mom was going through her own medical issues, and I had no support from my other family. I began to become more and more secluded, I just stayed to myself because I felt like a burden, and I felt like no one loved me. My brother Malcolm was a big reason why I felt this way. I felt that he was going to be there for me since our other brothers were gone in the military, and he wasn't.

One time when I had my T-tube he choked me because he was mad that one of his girlfriend's hurt him, Malcolm choked me again when he said that he was mad at me because he said I had more money than him, which was strange because my sister Marsha had control over the money I got from the car accident, and if he felt that way all he had to do was ask me for anything and I would have given it to him. I love my brothers and sisters; I'm the youngest in the family.

CHAPTER 12

"AGAIN, AND AGAIN"

When I got home, I was very sad, I just didn't like being there. Well after about three weeks at home my airway collapsed again and at this point I was just devastated. I was rushed to the hospital and Dr. Cotton was not happy, he didn't know what else to do.

Once again, as I always do, I started praying, I just cried asking God to please get me through this. Dr. Cotton met with my sister again to discuss options, and he strongly suggested that he put the T-tube back in my airway and just leave it there permanently, but my sister wasn't having that, so she decided that she wanted Dr. Cotton to do the tracheal resection again, yes, a third open chest operation.

So, Dr. Cotton explained the risks, infection and even death. So, they scheduled the surgery. This time I think they felt that this time it was a little more successful than the previous two because all the doctors said I did very well in surgery despite the risks. Back to intensive care I went, same feeding tube, chest tube, and staples to close my chest. I spent two weeks in intensive care.

CHAPTER 13

"THE NEAR-DEATH EXPERIENCE"

I was finally ready to go to the floor and I felt terrible. So, I got to the floor, and my chest was hurting really bad and I felt like I was going to throw up. The whole day I felt this way.

My nurse was Kim, one of my favorite nurses. She kept asking me how I felt and I told her I felt like I was going to vomit. Kim gave me an emesis basin in case I do throw up.

I began to feel a lot worse, and I started throwing up but it wasn't vomiting, it was blood that was coming up, globs and globs of it. Kim hit the code blue button in the room and all these doctors started running to my bedside, I started going in and out of consciousness, and I remembered looking up and seeing what looked like angels all around me.

So immediately I was rushed to the operating room where they opened my chest for the fourth time. What happened was my artery, which sat right next to my airway that supplies the right side of my brain with blood, erupted, it got infected and exploded. This artery also was near my heart. While in surgery I was bleeding a lot, the doctors thought that I was going to bleed to death because I was bleeding internally.

After surgery the doctors realized that all my previous operations that I had must have irritated that artery until it just gave out. Doctors told my family that I lost a lot of blood, not only in my body but also in my brain and that they were sure that I would have some kind of brain damage that would complicate the rest of my life.

So, I found myself back in intensive care and I had all kinds of tubes in both my nostrils, three IV's and of course a chest of tube. My chest was still open at the top there was just a gauze pad stuffed into a gaping hole at the top of my chest. I didn't feel much pain though; I guess because I was so drugged up.

CHAPTER 14

"ONLY GOD REMAINED"

I spent about three weeks in intensive care and the whole time I was just talking to God, thanking him for waking me up out of surgery.

When I left intensive care, I went back to the floor where I spent the next three weeks. I felt so alone, my family would visit but they wouldn't visit often and when they did visit it wasn't for very long and after a while I just didn't want them to visit at all, I didn't even want to go back home and that made me very sad at first, but after a while I knew I had a friend and a family in Jesus and he would supply my every need.

CHAPTER 15

"LIVING IN FEAR"

After spending more time in the hospital they released me to go home again and everything was just fine for the first couple of weeks, but the more I did and the more activity I attempted to do I began to feel more and more fatigued and the more I felt fatigued the more I began to get light headed, I mean at times my whole body would go numb.

I didn't tell anyone at first because I was scared that the doctors would cut me open again. So, I lived with this problem for about six months until I started to pass out. So, I went to see my doctors at a children's hospital, and they thought that I was faking, they just got upset every time I went to see them.

One doctor called me a hypochondriac, and other doctors just told me I was faking. So, after being told this for three years, I just thought that maybe they were right, maybe there wasn't anything wrong with me.

CHAPTER 16

"A NEW BEGINNING"

Soon I met the woman that would later become my wife, her name is Kali, and she was very supportive. About a year into our relationship, she noticed my symptoms, so I explained to her what I had been through in my life and told her that the doctors at Children's hospital believe that I am faking.

Kali suggested that I see a different doctor at a different hospital. I went to university hospital and there I saw Dr. Shauer and he took a special interest in my condition after seeing my medical history. Dr. Shauer at first diagnosed me with dementia because my memory was so bad and getting worse.

Dr. Shauer then wrote me a referral to a neurologist or brain specialist, her name is Dr. Bougabba. Dr. Bougabba ordered me to have a MRI & MRA and when I went to have this done, they told me that they would be taking pictures of my brain and my arteries leading to my brain.

I remember this day specifically because this was the day our country was attacked on 9/11. When the x-rays were taken and I was done in the imaging room I was told to wait in the waiting room so they could confirm my x-rays and in the waiting room me and the other patients were watching the news and that's when we saw the planes flying into the towers in New York.

After the test was done the man who read my pictures told me to contact my neurologist as soon as possible, so I asked him what was wrong and he told me that was all he could tell me and that I needed to contact my doctor as soon as I could, he told me to call my doctor before I even left the imaging center where they did the tests but I could not get in touch with her. So, I went home and called Dr. Bougabba and she told me that I needed to see her as soon as possible and that I could come to her office that day to discuss the results of the tests.

When I got to her office she did not hesitate to tell me what was wrong. Dr. Bougabba told me that the MRI and the MRA shows that I have a clot in my artery that supplies the right side of my brain with blood, she said that this means that the right side of my brain was not getting enough blood and that I would need to take blood thinners to dissolve the clot.

Dr. Bougabba told me that at first the pictures of my brain from the MRI made it seem as if I had a clot in my brain something she called some kind of dissection but as she looked at the MRI, she could clearly see that the clot was indeed in the artery and not my brain.

Next, Dr. Bougabba had me meet with a pharmacist about treatment. The pharmacist explained that he would be monitoring the medication because blood thinner medication is very dangerous if taken the wrong way. The name of the medication I would be taking is called coumadin (a blood thinner) but for the first two weeks I would have to give myself heparin injection, I had to give myself a shot twice a day for two weeks, then I would have to take the coumadin by mouth. I would have to take one and a half pills every other day and one pill the other day.

CHAPTER 17

"A SECOND CHANCE AT LIFE"

After setting up and talking with the pharmacist, Dr. Bougabba told me to see Dr. Shauer about work. The next day I saw Dr. Shauer and he told me that he felt that it would be best if I didn't return to work until they fixed my dizziness and passed out because I had explained to him the struggles I've experienced working because of dizziness and weakness and also passing out. I can't tell you how many jobs I have lost because of my medical history.

So, since I couldn't work, I decided to go to school and since I was now unable to work, I was given a Pell grant to go to college. I attended Southwestern College of Business where I majored in medical assisting which included courses in biology, pharmacology, medical terminology, anatomy and physiology, phlebotomy, medical assisting, computer keyboarding, and life skills.

I really enjoyed school especially since I really didn't have a school life after the accident. I did most of my schooling at home or in the hospital with a home tutor and the short time I was able to attend school I was talked about and ignored sometimes by my own brother and sister.

My father was killed in the accident, so I really didn't have a male figure around to help me or look up to. My brother Malcolm was around but most of the time he was out with different women or friends, he never really had time for me. Malcolm often took a lot of his frustrations out on me and twice tried to kill me by choking me and once while I had my T-tube.

CHAPTER 18

"LOST AND HOMELESS"

As I got older my brother Malcolm married and for a time, he let me stay with him and his family. I have to say that was one of the most brotherly things I can remember Malcolm ever doing for me.

My sister Ruthie was mean back then, she was embarrassed to be seen with me in public and I remember a time when I felt rejected by all my family living in Cincinnati so I went to my sister Ruthie because I had nowhere to go, but understand that I was in and out of the hospital a lot so at this time in my life I had to rely on my family.

I believe I was seventeen or eighteen at the time and I felt like I had no family. All I needed was a place to sleep so I asked Ruthie if I could sleep at her place. I told her that I just needed a place to sleep I would not just sit around her house I would leave as soon as I woke up and wouldn't return until I was ready to go back to sleep I didn't want anything from her but just a place to lay my head even if it was on her floor, I had nowhere else to go.

She said no, so I went downtown where I pretty much just walked around and looked around, not really knowing what to do. So, I started crying and praying, man I just felt lost and alone.

My next move was I went to an open interview at Kroger and was hired on the spot (praise God). So, after that I went back downtown where I pretty much stayed on fountain square. This was rough because I had nowhere to go so, I remember sitting down on a bench there on fountain square and I believe I fell asleep; this was like at some time really early in the morning when it was still dark outside. I remember a police officer waking me up and telling me I couldn't sleep there and he told me to leave.

I spent about a week downtown being homeless until I got my first paycheck from Kroger and then I had just enough money to pay for a motel room, sometimes I couldn't even afford to eat. There was a time when I was at work at Kroger and I just didn't know how I was going to get another bus card or how I was going to eat and while I was at work one night a lady came out of nowhere and handed me a dollar bill, I really didn't know what it was at first I just put it in my pocket, she just said someone told me you needed this and walked away, and I tell you it must have been God who sent her to me cause when I looked at that dollar bill later it was a fifty dollar bill, praise God, more than enough for what I needed.

CHAPTER 19

"PROOF OF PURPOSE"

I finished college with a 4.0gpa, pretty well for someone who wasn't expected to read a third-grade book, I am truly blessed. It was finally looking as if things were finally starting to go my way, I mean I graduated from college, my Mom and my fiancé and her family were there, and my daughter. Some of my aunts showed up and other past people in my life.

I don't speak much about my aunt's and uncle's because they hardly ever stayed in touch with me as I was going through my trials, but maybe that was my blessing because it certainly drew me closer to Jesus Christ who has always been everything I ever needed.

I will never be able to look at my aunt's and uncle's like I used to be able to again because after the accident they never really treated me like family and I know a lot of people have their opinions but from my standpoint, they made me feel as if I was not a part of the family.

CHAPTER 20

"NO IMPROVEMENT"

As time went on, despite the fact that I was being treated for the blood clot the doctor said she saw, I was still having dizzy spells and passing out.

After a little over a year of treatment I was instructed to go back to the imaging center for a repeat MRA, Dr. Bougabba only ordered an MRA this time since she knew the blockage was in the artery and not in my brain so she didn't need an MRI of my brain she just needed to look at my arteries.

After leaving the imaging center I went home to find a message on my answering machine telling me I had an appointment the following day to see Dr. Bougabba in her office to discuss the results of the MRA. The next day I went to the doctor's office for my appointment.

Dr. Bougabba informed me that the results of the MRA had not changed and that the treatment I had been under did not help, meaning that the coumadin (blood thinner) they were treating me with, which was meant to dissolve the clot, had not dissolved it at all. Dr. Bougabba said that the clot was the same size as it was when she originally discovered the problem and started treating it. She told me to continue taking the coumadin and that an appointment had been made for me to see Dr. Giglia, a vascular specialist.

CHAPTER 21

"SEARCHING FOR ANSWERS"

Two weeks later I went to see Dr. Giglia at the Christ hospital (mob) medical office building. Dr. Giglia introduced himself and explained to me what he does. After hearing what he was all about, he told me that he had gone over all my medical records and that he was amazed to see me doing as well as I was despite all that I had been through.

Dr. Giglia told me that he planned to take me to the operating room for a simple procedure that he explained would give him a better view of the artery that was blocked. This procedure would take about 30 to 35 minutes, he said. What he would do is take a long black, skinny wire with a camera at the tip of it to see the extent of the blockage.

I asked him, "How will you do this? Dr. Giglia said at the top of my leg, right on my inner thigh, in my groin area, he would make a small incision which would give him access to insert the wire to see arteries on that side of my body. Two weeks after the procedure was done, I was told to return to Dr. Giglia's office a week later to discuss the results.

CHAPTER 22

"THE TRUTH REVEALED"

A week later at Dr. Giglia's office, the results were in and it was not good. Dr. Giglia explained to my fiancé and me at the time Kali, that the clot that I was being treated for was not a clot, that it was in fact a stitch. He further explained that the stitch was more than likely a result of when my artery erupted and the doctors at Children's hospital more than likely stitched the artery off to prevent me from bleeding to death.

I asked, "was that the proper thing to do?" Dr. Giglia told me yes and no, he said that if they didn't stop the bleeding I more than likely would have bled to death. He said that they also stitched the artery off not taking into consideration that when they did that it cut off direct blood flow to the right side of my brain not considering the long-term effects of what they did.

As a result, that artery they stitched off cut off direct blood flow to the right side of my brain which meant that the right side of my brain was relying on the left side of my brain to supply it with blood and the more activity I did the less blood I got to the right side of my brain which was causing me to get light headed and pass out.

Dr. Giglia said that because of the procedure that cuts off blood flow to my brain and me living with that for more than four years, he said that he's surprised that I didn't have at least four or five strokes in that time period. Dr. Giglia explained that my condition was called Subclavian Steal Syndrome.

CHAPTER 23

"A RISKY SOLUTION"

Subclavian Steal Syndrome is most common in a person's arm or leg, Dr. Giglia said, that's why treatment is so risky in my case because it wasn't in either my arm or leg but in my carotid artery which runs through my chest and sat next to my airway and supplies the right side of my brain with blood.

Dr. Giglia said that he was exploring two options. One is that he could possibly place a stent into the artery to open it up so that the right side of my brain could receive a steady flow of blood, but he said that he felt that this procedure wouldn't completely fix the problem because he said that if the stint somehow got closed off or clogged with scar tissue or if blood just clotted off in the stint then I would be worse off than I was at that point.

The second option was to perform a bypass, which he felt would be the most effective way to fix the problem. Dr. Giglia explained that a bypass was very risky also but more than likely worked better in the long run, he later explained the procedure. It would involve a second surgeon, which would be the cardiothoracic surgeon to open my chest up so that he could operate. This was also a concern, because I had already had my chest cut open four times before.

Dr. Giglia said that after the cardio thoracic surgeon opened my chest, then he would go in to bypass the stitched artery. When he explained the procedure, it really upset Kali and she ran out of the room. I was devastated; I thought that most of my medical problems were over with.

CHAPTER 24

"THE DECISION OF FAITH"

I did the only thing I knew to do and that was pray. Dr. Giglia told me to think about what I wanted to do but told me to keep in mind while I thought about it that time was very important and that I needed to make a decision soon.

So, me and Kali left his office. Kali was upset and she told me that she didn't think I should go through with the operation, she said that if I survived this long then I could survive even longer but I explained to her that maybe that's the reason God revealed this condition now because maybe it was time to get it corrected. She was still upset and told me that even if I had the surgery there was no guarantee that it would fix the problem, but I told her that God didn't bring me this far for me to lose faith in him now and I told her that I was going to have the operation and she asked me, "how many times did I think I would be able to go through having my chest cut open, and that she would not be there to see me die."

So, she left me. I started praying and God revealed to me what needed to be done so I called Dr. Giglia and told him to schedule the operation. Then I called my Mom who was living in North Carolina at the time and told her that I was going to need her to come to Cincinnati to help me after surgery since Kali left, and of course Mom was right there. I felt so lost because all I could think about was my daughter Jazmine, and how much I was missing her at this time and how I had to get through this to get my fiancé and my daughter back.

CHAPTER 25

"HELP"

All thoughts of hope and redemption are gone. Trouble finds me no matter where I go. But that's life, I guess. No less of a man than the next. This life of mine is hexed.

A curse that life won't test. And you're telling me I'm blessed? An unachievable plan. This man is lost. Paid my do's. and it doesn't cover the cost. Time after time, I feel alone. You told me I would never be on my own. No matter what, hold on. But this flesh can't take much more. Saved me from the most daunting obstacles.

To live a life worth living. Knowing I gave you my best as a friend. If my life ended today, what could you do to me then? I'm here because of you. Because it was you who said that you would see me through. So now what do I do? When I've done all, can I? Please help me. Cause right now I can't stand it.

CHAPTER 26

"RESTORATION"

The operation went fine, God brought me through and answered my prayers once again, I even healed faster than they originally thought. I'm telling you God is truly awesome.

My fiancé came back and apologized to me maybe three or four weeks after the operation and that was all good. She even brought Jazmine to see me in the hospital.

My sister Ruthie is very close now, the way brother and sister should be. And to my aunt Ricky, the only aunt who truly treated me like family. I love you so much and thank you so much for all your help and support.

So now that I wasn't able to work, I applied for disability but was denied so I got a lawyer to help me. He was able to get my medical records and go to court about my medical history. While in court the judge after looking through all of my records ask the representative how they could deny someone with my medical history and the representative had no response so the judge ask my lawyer if I wanted to work because she saw that I had graduated from college so my lawyer asked me and I said yes as long as I was able to work I would so the judge ordered Social Security to pay me about 8 years of back pay that came out to be $22,000.

So, when I got my check, me and Kali got married on September 25th, 2002, my daughter Jazmine Asauda Tennyson was the flower girl. The wedding was small, it was just our Mothers, and Kali's sister, the pastor, and Jazmine there. We got married at her Mom's house. The following year my Son Jazail was born on July 16th, 2003. My prince was finally here. I was working in the microbiology lab at this time for the Health Alliance Department of the University of Cincinnati Hospital.

CHAPTER 27

"FORGIVENESS"

And finally, to everyone who asks me about how I feel about my family who wasn't there. I love every single one of them and if I could do anything to help them today I would.

They all played their part in my life. I just had to play mine.

"GOD BLESS EVERYONE"

ROLAND M. TENNYSON 'AUTHOR'